ICE HOCKEY
Journal

NAME ______________________________

SEASON YEAR ______________________________

TEAM NAME ______________________________

My Ice Hockey Journal

ICE HOCKEY *Journal* SECTIONS

01 Season Goals

Write down your Top 3 Season Goals

02 Training & Game Logbook

Record your training sessions and game details

03 Season Notes

Write further details of your season to keep a record for future reference

04 Autographs & Photos

Gather the autographs and photos of team members, coaches and famous players

01

SEASON GOALS

01 ICE HOCKEY SEASON GOALS

GOAL 1

....
....
....

GOAL 2

....
....
....

GOAL 3

....
....
....

My Ice Hockey Journal

-Ice Hockey-

02

TRAINING & GAME LOGBOOK

TRAINING

Date: / /

Start time :

End time :

Skills Completed

Write down the skills you worked on and developed during your training sessions

Skills to improve

Write down areas that you can improve on for your next training session

Coach & Team Focus

Write down if your coach or team has a skill or game focus you are working on

Extra Notes

Do you have additional notes or thoughts you would like to write down?

GAME DAY

Date: /   /   **Start time**   :

Location: ....

Home Game   **Away Game**

Game Details

.... **Vs** ....

Game Result

Goals   Goals

Our Score   Opposition Score

Coach Feedback

....

....

....

My Performance   Write down how you felt you contributed to the game. Did the coach provide you any personal feedback? Did you have any highlights? Did you have areas of improvement?

....

....

....

....

....

TRAINING

Date: / / **Start time** :

End time :

Skills Completed

Write down the skills you worked on and developed during your training sessions

....

....

....

....

Skills to improve

Write down areas that you can improve on for your next training session

....

....

....

....

Coach & Team Focus

Write down if your coach or team has a skill or game focus you are working on

....

....

Extra Notes

Do you have additional notes or thoughts you would like to write down?

....

....

....

GAME DAY

Date: /   /   **Start time**   :

Location: ....

Home Game   **Away Game**

Game Details

.... **Vs** ....

Game Result

Goals   Goals

Our Score   Opposition Score

Coach Feedback

....

....

....

My Performance   Write down how you felt you contributed to the game. Did the coach provide you any personal feedback? Did you have any highlights? Did you have areas of improvement?

....

....

....

....

....

TRAINING

Date: / /   **Start time** :

End time :

Skills Completed

Write down the skills you worked on and developed during your training sessions

....

....

....

....

Skills to improve

Write down areas that you can improve on for your next training session

....

....

....

....

Coach & Team Focus

Write down if your coach or team has a skill or game focus you are working on

....

....

Extra Notes

Do you have additional notes or thoughts you would like to write down?

....

....

....

GAME DAY

Date: /   /   **Start time**   :

Location: ....

Home Game   **Away Game**

Game Details

.... **Vs** ....

Game Result

Goals   Goals

Our Score   Opposition Score

Coach Feedback

....

....

....

My Performance

Write down how you felt you contributed to the game. Did the coach provide you any personal feedback? Did you have any highlights? Did you have areas of improvement?

....

....

....

....

....

....

TRAINING

Date: / / **Start time** :

End time :

Skills Completed

Write down the skills you worked on and developed during your training sessions

....

....

....

....

Skills to improve

Write down areas that you can improve on for your next training session

....

....

....

....

Coach & Team Focus

Write down if your coach or team has a skill or game focus you are working on

....

....

Extra Notes

Do you have additional notes or thoughts you would like to write down?

....

....

....

GAME DAY

Date: / /   **Start time**   :

Location: ....

Home Game   **Away Game**

Game Details

.... **Vs** ....

Game Result

                    Goals   Goals

Our Score   Opposition Score

Coach Feedback

....

....

....

My Performance   Write down how you felt you contributed to the game. Did the coach provide you any personal feedback? Did you have any highlights? Did you have areas of improvement?

....

....

....

....

....

TRAINING

Date: / / **Start time** :

End time :

Skills Completed

Write down the skills you worked on and developed during your training sessions

....

....

....

....

Skills to improve

Write down areas that you can improve on for your next training session

....

....

....

....

Coach & Team Focus

Write down if your coach or team has a skill or game focus you are working on

....

....

Extra Notes

Do you have additional notes or thoughts you would like to write down?

....

....

....

GAME DAY

Date: /   /

Start time   :

Location: ....

Home Game   **Away Game**

Game Details

.... **Vs** ....

Game Result

Goals   Goals

Our Score   Opposition Score

Coach Feedback

....

....

....

My Performance

Write down how you felt you contributed to the game. Did the coach provide you any personal feedback? Did you have any highlights? Did you have areas of improvement?

....

....

....

....

....

....

TRAINING

Date: / /   **Start time** :

End time :

Skills Completed

Write down the skills you worked on and developed during your training sessions

....

....

....

....

Skills to improve

Write down areas that you can improve on for your next training session

....

....

....

....

Coach & Team Focus

Write down if your coach or team has a skill or game focus you are working on

....

....

Extra Notes

Do you have additional notes or thoughts you would like to write down?

....

....

....

GAME DAY

Date:　　/　　/　　　　**Start time**　　　**:**

Location: ....

Home Game　　　　**Away Game**

Game Details

.... **Vs** ....

Game Result

　　　　　　Goals　　　　　　　　　　Goals

Our Score　　　　　Opposition Score

Coach Feedback

....

....

....

My Performance

Write down how you felt you contributed to the game. Did the coach provide you any personal feedback? Did you have any highlights? Did you have areas of improvement?

....

....

....

....

....

TRAINING

Date: / /   **Start time** :

End time :

Skills Completed

Write down the skills you worked on and developed during your training sessions

....

....

....

....

Skills to improve

Write down areas that you can improve on for your next training session

....

....

....

....

Coach & Team Focus

Write down if your coach or team has a skill or game focus you are working on

....

....

Extra Notes

Do you have additional notes or thoughts you would like to write down?

....

....

....

GAME DAY

Date: /   /   **Start time**   :

Location: ....

Home Game   **Away Game**

Game Details

.... **Vs** ....

Game Result

               Goals   Goals

Our Score   Opposition Score

Coach Feedback

....

....

....

My Performance   Write down how you felt you contributed to the game. Did the coach provide you any personal feedback? Did you have any highlights? Did you have areas of improvement?

....

....

....

....

....

....

TRAINING

Date: / /   **Start time** :

End time :

Skills Completed

Write down the skills you worked on and developed during your training sessions

....

....

....

....

Skills to improve

Write down areas that you can improve on for your next training session

....

....

....

....

Coach & Team Focus

Write down if your coach or team has a skill or game focus you are working on

....

....

Extra Notes

Do you have additional notes or thoughts you would like to write down?

....

....

....

GAME DAY

Date: /   /   **Start time**   :

Location: ....

Home Game   **Away Game**

Game Details

.... **Vs** ....

Game Result

Goals   Goals

Our Score   Opposition Score

Coach Feedback

....

....

....

My Performance   Write down how you felt you contributed to the game. Did the coach provide you any personal feedback? Did you have any highlights? Did you have areas of improvement?

....

....

....

....

....

TRAINING

Date: / /   **Start time** :

End time :

Skills Completed

Write down the skills you worked on and developed during your training sessions

....

....

....

....

Skills to improve

Write down areas that you can improve on for your next training session

....

....

....

....

Coach & Team Focus

Write down if your coach or team has a skill or game focus you are working on

....

....

Extra Notes

Do you have additional notes or thoughts you would like to write down?

....

....

....

GAME DAY

Date: /   /   **Start time**   :

Location: ....

Home Game   **Away Game**

Game Details

.... **Vs** ....

Game Result

Goals   Goals

Our Score   Opposition Score

Coach Feedback

....

....

....

My Performance Write down how you felt you contributed to the game. Did the coach provide you any personal feedback? Did you have any highlights? Did you have areas of improvement?

....

....

....

....

....

TRAINING

Date: / /   **Start time** :

End time :

Skills Completed
Write down the skills you worked on and developed during your training sessions

....

....

....

....

Skills to improve
Write down areas that you can improve on for your next training session

....

....

....

....

Coach & Team Focus
Write down if your coach or team has a skill or game focus you are working on

....

....

Extra Notes
Do you have additional notes or thoughts you would like to write down?

....

....

....

GAME DAY

Date: /   /   **Start time**   :

Location: ....

Home Game   **Away Game**

Game Details

.... **Vs** ....

Game Result

           Goals   Goals

Our Score   Opposition Score

Coach Feedback

....
....
....

My Performance   Write down how you felt you contributed to the game. Did the coach provide you any personal feedback? Did you have any highlights? Did you have areas of improvement?

....
....
....
....
....
....

TRAINING

Date: / / 　　**Start time** :

　　End time :

Skills Completed

Write down the skills you worked on and developed during your training sessions

....

....

....

....

Skills to improve

Write down areas that you can improve on for your next training session

....

....

....

Coach & Team Focus

Write down if your coach or team has a skill or game focus you are working on

....

....

Extra Notes

Do you have additional notes or thoughts you would like to write down?

....

....

....

GAME DAY

Date: /   /   **Start time**   :

Location: ....

Home Game   **Away Game**

Game Details

.... **Vs** ....

Game Result

              Goals   Goals

Our Score   Opposition Score

Coach Feedback

....

....

....

My Performance

Write down how you felt you contributed to the game. Did the coach provide you any personal feedback? Did you have any highlights? Did you have areas of improvement?

....

....

....

....

....

....

TRAINING

Date: / /   **Start time**   :

End time   :

Skills Completed
Write down the skills you worked on and developed during your training sessions

....

....

....

....

Skills to improve
Write down areas that you can improve on for your next training session

....

....

....

....

Coach & Team Focus
Write down if your coach or team has a skill or game focus you are working on

....

....

Extra Notes
Do you have additional notes or thoughts you would like to write down?

....

....

....

GAME DAY

Date: /   /   **Start time**   :

Location: ....

Home Game   **Away Game**

Game Details

.... **Vs** ....

Game Result

Goals   Goals

Our Score   Opposition Score

Coach Feedback

....

....

....

My Performance   Write down how you felt you contributed to the game. Did the coach provide you any personal feedback? Did you have any highlights? Did you have areas of improvement?

....

....

....

....

....

TRAINING

Date: / / **Start time** :

End time :

Skills Completed

Write down the skills you worked on and developed during your training sessions

....

....

....

....

Skills to improve

Write down areas that you can improve on for your next training session

....

....

....

....

Coach & Team Focus

Write down if your coach or team has a skill or game focus you are working on

....

....

Extra Notes

Do you have additional notes or thoughts you would like to write down?

....

....

....

GAME DAY

Date: / / **Start time** :

Location: ....

Home Game **Away Game**

Game Details

.... **Vs** ....

Game Result

Goals Goals

Our Score Opposition Score

Coach Feedback

....
....
....

My Performance Write down how you felt you contributed to the game. Did the coach provide you any personal feedback? Did you have any highlights? Did you have areas of improvement?

....
....
....
....
....
....

TRAINING

Date: / /   **Start time** :

End time :

Skills Completed

Write down the skills you worked on and developed during your training sessions

....

....

....

....

Skills to improve

Write down areas that you can improve on for your next training session

....

....

....

....

Coach & Team Focus

Write down if your coach or team has a skill or game focus you are working on

....

....

Extra Notes

Do you have additional notes or thoughts you would like to write down?

....

....

....

GAME DAY

Date: / / **Start time** :

Location: ....

Home Game   **Away Game**

Game Details

.... **Vs** ....

Game Result

Goals   Goals

Our Score   Opposition Score

Coach Feedback

....

....

....

My Performance   Write down how you felt you contributed to the game. Did the coach provide you any personal feedback? Did you have any highlights? Did you have areas of improvement?

....

....

....

....

....

TRAINING

Date: / /

Start time :

End time :

Skills Completed

Write down the skills you worked on and developed during your training sessions

....

....

....

....

Skills to improve

Write down areas that you can improve on for your next training session

....

....

....

....

Coach & Team Focus

Write down if your coach or team has a skill or game focus you are working on

....

....

Extra Notes

Do you have additional notes or thoughts you would like to write down?

....

....

....

GAME DAY

Date: /   /   **Start time**   :

Location: ....

Home Game   **Away Game**

Game Details

.... **Vs** ....

Game Result

Goals   Goals

Our Score   Opposition Score

Coach Feedback

....

....

....

My Performance   Write down how you felt you contributed to the game. Did the coach provide you any personal feedback? Did you have any highlights? Did you have areas of improvement?

....

....

....

....

....

....

TRAINING

Date: / /   **Start time**   :

End time   :

Skills Completed

Write down the skills you worked on and developed during your training sessions

....

....

....

....

Skills to improve

Write down areas that you can improve on for your next training session

....

....

....

....

Coach & Team Focus

Write down if your coach or team has a skill or game focus you are working on

....

....

Extra Notes

Do you have additional notes or thoughts you would like to write down?

....

....

....

GAME DAY

Date: /   /   **Start time**   :

Location: ....

Home Game   **Away Game**

Game Details

.... **Vs** ....

Game Result

Goals   Goals

Our Score   Opposition Score

Coach Feedback

....

....

....

My Performance Write down how you felt you contributed to the game. Did the coach provide you any personal feedback? Did you have any highlights? Did you have areas of improvement?

....

....

....

....

....

TRAINING

Date: / /

Start time :

End time :

Skills Completed

Write down the skills you worked on and developed during your training sessions

....

....

....

....

Skills to improve

Write down areas that you can improve on for your next training session

....

....

....

....

Coach & Team Focus

Write down if your coach or team has a skill or game focus you are working on

....

....

Extra Notes

Do you have additional notes or thoughts you would like to write down?

....

....

....

GAME DAY

Date: /   /   **Start time**   :

Location: ....

Home Game   **Away Game**

Game Details

.... **Vs** ....

Game Result

Goals   Goals

Our Score   Opposition Score

Coach Feedback

....

....

....

My Performance

Write down how you felt you contributed to the game. Did the coach provide you any personal feedback? Did you have any highlights? Did you have areas of improvement?

....

....

....

....

....

....

TRAINING

Date: / /

Start time :

End time :

Skills Completed

Write down the skills you worked on and developed during your training sessions

....

....

....

....

Skills to improve

Write down areas that you can improve on for your next training session

....

....

....

....

Coach & Team Focus

Write down if your coach or team has a skill or game focus you are working on

....

....

Extra Notes

Do you have additional notes or thoughts you would like to write down?

....

....

....

GAME DAY

Date: / /   **Start time**   :

Location: ....

Home Game   **Away Game**

Game Details

.... **Vs** ....

Game Result

Goals   Goals

Our Score   Opposition Score

Coach Feedback

....

....

....

My Performance   Write down how you felt you contributed to the game. Did the coach provide you any personal feedback? Did you have any highlights? Did you have areas of improvement?

....

....

....

....

....

TRAINING

Date: / /   **Start time** :

End time :

Skills Completed

Write down the skills you worked on and developed during your training sessions

....

....

....

....

Skills to improve

Write down areas that you can improve on for your next training session

....

....

....

....

Coach & Team Focus

Write down if your coach or team has a skill or game focus you are working on

....

....

Extra Notes

Do you have additional notes or thoughts you would like to write down?

....

....

....

GAME DAY

Date: /   /   **Start time**   :

Location: ....

Home Game   **Away Game**

Game Details

.... **Vs** ....

Game Result

              Goals   Goals

Our Score   Opposition Score

Coach Feedback

....

....

....

My Performance   Write down how you felt you contributed to the game. Did the coach provide you any personal feedback? Did you have any highlights? Did you have areas of improvement?

....

....

....

....

....

....

TRAINING

Date: / /

Start time :

End time :

Skills Completed

Write down the skills you worked on and developed during your training sessions

Skills to improve

Write down areas that you can improve on for your next training session

Coach & Team Focus

Write down if your coach or team has a skill or game focus you are working on

Extra Notes

Do you have additional notes or thoughts you would like to write down?

GAME DAY

Date: / /   **Start time**   :

Location: ....

Home Game   **Away Game**

Game Details

.... **Vs** ....

Game Result

Goals   Goals

Our Score   Opposition Score

Coach Feedback

....

....

....

My Performance

Write down how you felt you contributed to the game. Did the coach provide you any personal feedback? Did you have any highlights? Did you have areas of improvement?

....

....

....

....

....

TRAINING

Date: / /   **Start time** :

End time :

Skills Completed

Write down the skills you worked on and developed during your training sessions

....

....

....

....

Skills to improve

Write down areas that you can improve on for your next training session

....

....

....

....

Coach & Team Focus

Write down if your coach or team has a skill or game focus you are working on

....

....

Extra Notes

Do you have additional notes or thoughts you would like to write down?

....

....

....

GAME DAY

Date: /   /   **Start time**   :

Location: ....

Home Game   **Away Game**

Game Details

.... **Vs** ....

Game Result

Goals   Goals

Our Score   Opposition Score

Coach Feedback

....

....

....

My Performance   Write down how you felt you contributed to the game. Did the coach provide you any personal feedback? Did you have any highlights? Did you have areas of improvement?

....

....

....

....

....

....

TRAINING

Date: / /   **Start time**   :

End time   :

Skills Completed

Write down the skills you worked on and developed during your training sessions

....

....

....

....

Skills to improve

Write down areas that you can improve on for your next training session

....

....

....

....

Coach & Team Focus

Write down if your coach or team has a skill or game focus you are working on

....

....

Extra Notes

Do you have additional notes or thoughts you would like to write down?

....

....

....

GAME DAY

Date: /   /   **Start time**   :

Location: ....

Home Game   **Away Game**

Game Details

.... **Vs** ....

Game Result

                    Goals   Goals

Our Score   Opposition Score

Coach Feedback

....

....

....

My Performance   Write down how you felt you contributed to the game. Did the coach provide you any personal feedback? Did you have any highlights? Did you have areas of improvement?

....

....

....

....

....

TRAINING

Date: / /   **Start time**   :

End time   :

Skills Completed

Write down the skills you worked on and developed during your training sessions

....

....

....

....

Skills to improve

Write down areas that you can improve on for your next training session

....

....

....

....

Coach & Team Focus

Write down if your coach or team has a skill or game focus you are working on

....

....

Extra Notes

Do you have additional notes or thoughts you would like to write down?

....

....

....

GAME DAY

Date: /   /   **Start time**   :

Location: ....

Home Game   **Away Game**

Game Details

.... **Vs** ....

Game Result

Goals   Goals

Our Score   Opposition Score

Coach Feedback

....
....
....

My Performance   Write down how you felt you contributed to the game. Did the coach provide you any personal feedback? Did you have any highlights? Did you have areas of improvement?

....
....
....
....
....

TRAINING

Date: / /   **Start time**   :

End time   :

Skills Completed

Write down the skills you worked on and developed during your training sessions

....

....

....

....

Skills to improve

Write down areas that you can improve on for your next training session

....

....

....

....

Coach & Team Focus

Write down if your coach or team has a skill or game focus you are working on

....

....

Extra Notes

Do you have additional notes or thoughts you would like to write down?

....

....

....

GAME DAY

Date: / /   **Start time**   :

Location: ....

Home Game   **Away Game**

Game Details

.... **Vs** ....

Game Result

Goals   Goals

Our Score   Opposition Score

Coach Feedback

....

....

....

My Performance   Write down how you felt you contributed to the game. Did the coach provide you any personal feedback? Did you have any highlights? Did you have areas of improvement?

....

....

....

....

....

TRAINING

Date: / /   **Start time**   :

End time   :

Skills Completed

Write down the skills you worked on and developed during your training sessions

Skills to improve

Write down areas that you can improve on for your next training session

Coach & Team Focus

Write down if your coach or team has a skill or game focus you are working on

Extra Notes

Do you have additional notes or thoughts you would like to write down?

GAME DAY

Date: /   /   **Start time**   :

Location: ....

Home Game   **Away Game**

Game Details

.... **Vs** ....

Game Result

                    Goals   Goals

Our Score   Opposition Score

Coach Feedback

....

....

....

My Performance   Write down how you felt you contributed to the game. Did the coach provide you any personal feedback? Did you have any highlights? Did you have areas of improvement?

....

....

....

....

....

....

TRAINING

Date: / /   **Start time**   :

End time   :

Skills Completed

Write down the skills you worked on and developed during your training sessions

....

....

....

....

Skills to improve

Write down areas that you can improve on for your next training session

....

....

....

....

Coach & Team Focus

Write down if your coach or team has a skill or game focus you are working on

....

....

Extra Notes

Do you have additional notes or thoughts you would like to write down?

....

....

....

GAME DAY 

Date: /   /   **Start time**   :

Location: ....

Home Game   **Away Game**

Game Details

.... **Vs** ....

Game Result

                    Goals   Goals

Our Score   Opposition Score

Coach Feedback

....

....

....

My Performance

Write down how you felt you contributed to the game. Did the coach provide you any personal feedback? Did you have any highlights? Did you have areas of improvement?

....

....

....

....

....

TRAINING

Date: /   /

Start time   :

End time   :

Skills Completed

Write down the skills you worked on and developed during your training sessions

Skills to improve

Write down areas that you can improve on for your next training session

Coach & Team Focus

Write down if your coach or team has a skill or game focus you are working on

Extra Notes

Do you have additional notes or thoughts you would like to write down?

GAME DAY

Date: /   /   **Start time**   :

Location: ....

Home Game   **Away Game**

Game Details

.... **Vs** ....

Game Result

                    Goals   Goals

Our Score   Opposition Score

Coach Feedback

....

....

....

My Performance

Write down how you felt you contributed to the game. Did the coach provide you any personal feedback? Did you have any highlights? Did you have areas of improvement?

....

....

....

....

....

....

TRAINING

Date: / /   **Start time**   :

End time   :

Skills Completed

Write down the skills you worked on and developed during your training sessions

Skills to improve

Write down areas that you can improve on for your next training session

Coach & Team Focus

Write down if your coach or team has a skill or game focus you are working on

Extra Notes

Do you have additional notes or thoughts you would like to write down?

GAME DAY

Date: / /   **Start time**   :

Location: ....

Home Game   **Away Game**

Game Details

.... **Vs** ....

Game Result

Goals   Goals

Our Score   Opposition Score

Coach Feedback

....

....

....

My Performance   Write down how you felt you contributed to the game. Did the coach provide you any personal feedback? Did you have any highlights? Did you have areas of improvement?

....

....

....

....

....

TRAINING

Date: / /   **Start time**   :

End time   :

Skills Completed

Write down the skills you worked on and developed during your training sessions

....

....

....

....

Skills to improve

Write down areas that you can improve on for your next training session

....

....

....

Coach & Team Focus

Write down if your coach or team has a skill or game focus you are working on

....

....

Extra Notes

Do you have additional notes or thoughts you would like to write down?

....

....

....

GAME DAY

Date: /   /   **Start time**   :

Location: ....

Home Game   **Away Game**

Game Details

.... **Vs** ....

Game Result

                Goals   Goals

Our Score   Opposition Score

Coach Feedback

....
....
....

My Performance   Write down how you felt you contributed to the game. Did the coach provide you any personal feedback? Did you have any highlights? Did you have areas of improvement?

....
....
....
....
....

TRAINING

Date: / /   **Start time** :

End time :

Skills Completed

Write down the skills you worked on and developed during your training sessions

....

....

....

....

Skills to improve

Write down areas that you can improve on for your next training session

....

....

....

....

Coach & Team Focus

Write down if your coach or team has a skill or game focus you are working on

....

....

Extra Notes

Do you have additional notes or thoughts you would like to write down?

....

....

....

GAME DAY

Date: /   /   **Start time**   :

Location: ....

Home Game   **Away Game**

Game Details

.... **Vs** ....

Game Result

            Goals   Goals

Our Score   Opposition Score

Coach Feedback

....
....
....

My Performance

Write down how you felt you contributed to the game. Did the coach provide you any personal feedback? Did you have any highlights? Did you have areas of improvement?

....
....
....
....
....

TRAINING

Date: / /

Start time :

End time :

Skills Completed

Write down the skills you worked on and developed during your training sessions

....

....

....

....

Skills to improve

Write down areas that you can improve on for your next training session

....

....

....

....

Coach & Team Focus

Write down if your coach or team has a skill or game focus you are working on

....

....

Extra Notes

Do you have additional notes or thoughts you would like to write down?

....

....

....

GAME DAY

Date:　　/　　/　　　　**Start time**　　　　:

Location: ....

Home Game　　　　**Away Game**

Game Details

.... **Vs** ....

Game Result

　　　　　　Goals　　　　　　　　　　　　　Goals

Our Score　　　　　　Opposition Score

Coach Feedback

....

....

....

My Performance

Write down how you felt you contributed to the game. Did the coach provide you any personal feedback? Did you have any highlights? Did you have areas of improvement?

....

....

....

....

....

....

TRAINING

Date: / /   **Start time** :

End time :

Skills Completed
Write down the skills you worked on and developed during your training sessions

....

....

....

....

Skills to improve
Write down areas that you can improve on for your next training session

....

....

....

....

Coach & Team Focus
Write down if your coach or team has a skill or game focus you are working on

....

....

Extra Notes
Do you have additional notes or thoughts you would like to write down?

....

....

....

GAME DAY

Date: /   /   **Start time**   :

Location: ....

Home Game   **Away Game**

Game Details

.... **Vs** ....

Game Result

                    Goals   Goals

Our Score   Opposition Score

Coach Feedback

....

....

....

My Performance Write down how you felt you contributed to the game. Did the coach provide you any personal feedback? Did you have any highlights? Did you have areas of improvement?

....

....

....

....

....

My Ice Hockey Journal

-Ice Hockey-

03

SEASON NOTES

NOTES

NOTES 

My Ice Hockey Journal

-Ice Hockey-

04

Autographs & Photos

Autographs & Photo's

Autographs & Photo's

Autographs & Photo's

Autographs & Photo's

Autographs & Photo's

ICE HOCKEY

Journal

The Life Graduate
PUBLISHING GROUP

-Ice Hockey-